A Poet's Sketch of His Biography

By the Same Author

ISLANDS OF EXPERIENCE

A Poet's Sketch

of His Biography

Dean Nichols

Resource *Publications*

An imprint of *Wipf and Stock Publishers*
199 West 8th Avenue • Eugene OR 97401

Resource Publications
A division of Wipf and Stock Publishers
199 W 8th Ave, Suite 3
Eugene, OR 97401

A Poet's Sketch of His Biography
By Nichols, Dean
Copyright©1979 by Nichols, Dean
ISBN: 1-59244-876-3
Publication date 9/24/2004
Previously published by Exposition Press, 1979

To Inez,
who bore me
and gave me words

To Laura,
who understood me
and loved me still

"... Lord, to whom
shall we go?
Thou hast the words
of eternal life"

Contents

Acknowledgments

My thanks go to the people, but especially the fishermen, of Cordova, Alaska, who understand that the open and frank things we say about others, when said with love, are a vital part of any real expression of that love.

And to the many who encouraged, even prodded, me by insisting, "Dean, it is time for your second book."

And to Alma June, who quietly agreed.

*   *   *

THIS IS NOT a religious book, although I have become a Christian. But it took me fifty-two sometimes dull, often wearying, occasionally adventure-filled, frequently puzzling years to become a real one. Always I carried somewhere in my being the awe at knowing I am a creation of God's and therefore eternal, indestructible, and limited only by my imagination, daring, and faith. This book simply presents some of a poet's sketches those years produced.

Most were written before I fully and truly acknowledged Jesus as my own personal Savior and Lord, so a few will show that I knew the world. But even so, most of those written before my spiritual birthday, February 19, 1972, will show that my soul heard Him calling my name for some years. I'm glad I finally stopped running and just stood still and accepted Him.

A dear friend and sister in Christ had done some kind things for me, so I gave her a copy of my book, *Islands Of Experience*. I wrote some appreciative words on the autograph page and then slipped in and laid it on her desk while she was away. She claims she has never written anything but grocery lists, but after you read the following poem of thanks, I believe you'll agree with me, they must be some grocery lists.

A Sign of Caring

I found a treasure yesterday. . . .

We treasure things that are given to us by others,
because giving is a sign of caring—

For human beings,
knowing that someone cared enough to give
is a thrilling yet comforting thought.

Many people—when they think of giving—think of
money;
"What can I buy to show I care?"

But the most treasured things on earth are
without money
and
without price:

Dew drops on the grass, a bird's early morning song,
tiny forget-me-not flowers, a sky
wrapped in a crimson sunset—
all of these treasures given to us
by God—
    Who cares for us.

    Sometimes . . . people give of themselves—give
their time to help a friend . . . or give something
they have made.
    Others write lovely books full of beautiful thoughts
(and leave a copy on a friend's desk—and when she
finds it, she feels that she has found a treasure).
    Giving such a book, an author gives a little bit
of himself with it.
    I found a treasure yesterday. . . .
    A touching book of poetry. I wanted to offer to pay
for it, but I realized that it would no longer be
a gift and so would lose some of its value—and, too,
paying would destroy for you the joy of giving.
    Thank you, brother, thank you.

GRACE MITCHELL
Pastor's Secretary
Bible Baptist Church
Anchorage, Alaska
June 14, 1974

LAURA

Even the most discriminating connoisseur would not expect to find a perfect wine, for that would end his searching.

Instead, he spends his life seeking the best, and that best only for a special occasion, or the best from a certain vine. Always there is margin for improvement; and that is what makes the difference.

A Glass of Rare Wine
(Vintage 1893)

Who is this youth with the fresh ideas,
the vibrant, exciting view of life?
Who is this person whose sage wisdom
has grown from the years?

Who is this woman who has known a thousand storms,
yet who thrills to a new storm
because it is new?

Who is this child who sees today and tomorrow
as the most exciting days of all,
because only they can hold promise?

Who is she who knows no age
because she knows the timelessness
of beauty and love?

Who is my love who sets me free
from the only chains that can bind me,
those I place upon myself;
who is she who sets me free
just by her love?

Who is this glass of rare wine,
filled to its sparkling edge
    with fresh, vibrant youth tempered with years,
    with the challenge of a storm yet with the daring
to thrill and laugh in the face of the storm;
    with the promise of tomorrow built
on the wonder of today;
    with the intensity of now amplified
by the timelessness of time;
    with freedom from the only jailer, self;
who is she?

Well let me say, to me
she is an aunt, a friend,
a teacher, a student,
a confessor, a confidante,
a guiding rod of iron,
a unique and special creation by the hand of God
made all the more lovable by her possession
of the human frailties that make her of the earth;

Her name is Laura.

December 15, 1969

To Laura, from all who knew and loved her

She Loved Me

I am going to the grave
of my father's sister;
I am going—to bury Laura.
But I'm going to say goodbye
to more than an old friend,
more even than one of my own blood.

You see, she loved me.
Since beyond years I can't remember
she loved me.
Whether I was riding the clouds of glory
or dredging the depths of despair;
whether I was pure and perfect
and singing the praises of our Lord,
or twisted and dirty
and questioning His very name,
she loved me.

And when I knew,
more than any of His creatures,
that I was unworthy
even of His pity,
she loved me.
I have never talked to Jesus;
I have never seen Him face to face;
but I knew Laura.

If she had imperfections
(she must have had,
    for she was of the earth)
I never knew them;

for no matter what the storms
that tore into her life;
no matter how she battled deep within,
or fought the enemy
where all the world could see,
I know for me
one single ray of light,
one tiny flame burned on which said
she loved me.

And He
　　　created Laura.

　　　　　　Somewhere in the night sky
　　　　　　flying from where she was born
　　　　　　to where she died.
　　　　　　October 19, 1973

ALASKA

Will You Listen?

Will you listen to my song
    if I sing to you?
I'm not a robin, spreading the forest with notes
tumbling all over each other;
I'm not a thrush, whose long song
fills the spaces as completely
as the breeze fills the spaces
between the evergreen boughs;
nor am I that breeze brushing the trees
and singing the soft and soothing song
that breezes sing.

I am but a man;
and my song is words.
And though intelligence and denotation
are the burden of words,
sometimes, instead, I'd have them sing
and spread their message like a robin's song,

challenging your mind to put together
the fascinating puzzle
that is clearly there.

Sometimes I'd have them sing
as the thrush would sing,
filling the spaces
so that you feel complete,
knowing that the message feeds your heart
even though the mind cares not to comprehend.

And then sometimes
I'd have them sing as the breezes sing,
no notes, no messages,
but only soft and soothing sounds
that reach into the soul
and do not tell at all,
but rather, leave that quiet, deep awareness:
    all is well.

But I must sing
as surely as the birds must sing
or breeze must blow.
I must sing.
Will you listen?

July-September, 1971

20

It may be of interest to readers to know a bit of the history that is the basis for the poetic expression that follows this.

I was raised on the banks of the Columbia River in Washington State and grew up in river work. Although I graduated from high school in 1938 into a full-time tugboat skipper's job, the many previous summers were also spent in long hours of log booming and boat work.

In December of 1954 I responded to the urge to stay ashore and took a job as an assistant to the electrical engineer at the local utility. But that wore thin and in March of 1958 I found myself in Anchorage, Alaska, working as a radio communicator for the Federal Aviation Agency.

As the poem points out, I left the FAA in April of 1965 to work for six months as a Protection/Boat Officer for the Alaska Department of Fish and Game out of Cordova. The following spring the ADF&G found that they could not offer me a full six months of work again that year, so rather than take a much-shortened season, I applied again for work with the FAA.

At the writing of *A Poet's Sketch* . . . I was awaiting assignment to the FAA station at Bettles, on the slopes of the Brooks Range, twenty-five miles north of the Arctic Circle.

A Poet's Sketch of His Biography

A river man was I. The broad Columbia held me close within her arms; nor was I one to leave. I loved her as I knew that she loved me. And, as I now recall, I knew I'd never leave her.

No ocean wide for me. It was not fear that kept me from the sea but love for one who nursed me on her knee from waters rich in history; who told me stories, with her sighing winds and washing waves and lush green forests on her banks and mountains rising high; who told me stories of the hidden past, and from the challenge of the ones before, stirred deep within the urge to write my page in history here on the broad Columbia's way.

But oh, the fickle compass of our day. I took a course and found myself dashed high upon the shore. The siren call of science held me for three years; three years of guiding people in the use of unseen energy. The wonder of electric power was such a force as blinded me to memory of my old love.

21

And still the siren call of science reached for me by adding yet another call, the call to roam. The airplane and its magic wings, the unseen power of radio with voices of so many men I'll never see, the lure of the last frontier; these all combined and led me to the north, and gone forever, broken into dreams, a love affair is now a story of the past, one day a legend, if indeed it e'er will last.

But love is strange and powerful. Alaska's call, her mountains tall, her ridges frosted to the sky, the big broad land with spirit coursing with the breeze, the waters, waters everywhere and room to breathe, these too combined to capture heart and soul, and deep in love I fell; Alaska's son from some pre-life has now come home.

For seven years I watched the winged things fly into sky that reached to everywhere; for seven years I talked to men by radio from Greenland clear to Tokyo and knew the joy and sweat and pain of service to these men from many lands.

But deep within the ashes of the past a coal burned; a fire not dead though covered by the ash of time. And from the pages of the magazines of boats and engines and the endless sea, there sprang a breeze that blew away the ash and fanned to flame the one remaining ember there, the call of the open sea.

And so I left the science and the wings and dashed headlong into the arms of one small boat, the Copper Sands and deep Prince William Sound. Oh, there were times of fear and sweat, and dull and aching limbs, but those were passing shadows of the clouds. I was the master of a ship—who cares how small? I dared the open sea and felt the awe and freedom all as one. I saw the thundering combers on the bars and felt relief, and yes, some victory, drain out the tension and the fear when safe inside. I heard the wind roar fearful threats high on the hill until its voice grew hoarse and only whispered, and all the while I lay at anchor in a tiny and protected cove and reveled in the joy of those protecting arms.

And then the winds of fate blew down my course. No matter how I tacked and strove, I could not gain. Fate's ugly hand (or so it seems to me in blindness now) points yet another way.

Not only to the shore she points, with finger strong and fixed with firm command, but far inland past beaches and the bars, past rivers wide, o'er tundra and the muskeg far till stand I must and look straight up to see the great North Star.

So now the story ends for simple reason that no more can here be written down till more is lived.

I wonder, as I wait my turn to serve my time far up the northern slope, if God has left some room for hope that the burning coal of fire will be preserved to spring to flame again one day and call me to the wonder of the awesome, endless sea whereon the soul of man stands tall and free.

Summer 1966

The Wind

When the cold wind blows in the northland,
and the hoar frost falls to the ground,
and the rustling breeze in the frozen trees
has a silent yet ominous sound;

I know who my enemy is here,
who holds the real power to kill;
and it isn't the cold and the snow here,
nor the ice fog, drifting and still.

And it isn't the night with its eerie light,
nor the cold slanting sun in the day,
nor the lonely press of the wilderness
whose silence defies you to pray.

It's the wind with its claws and its hunger
for all that is life to your bones.
It's the wind that steals till your life blood feels
the ice crystals form in your veins.

For heat is your life in the northland.
Without it you're crystal and stone;
and the claws of the wind would reach under your skin
to ravage what little you own.

December 1962

I have never actually lived in a sod-roofed cabin; but I have seen them in their peaceful setting, and I have understood why they were built and why they were lived in there. They have told me the following little story.

Heaven

I found heaven in the tundra;
I found peace and stillness there,
in a cabin built of logs and sod
with barrel stove and chair,

And a cache on poles where I can store
my grub and other stuff,
that friendly Bruin could assume
is his, and treat it rough.

I found heaven in the tundra,
where the trees are scrub and small,
but the silence so enormous
I can't help but feel its call

To listen to my heart and soul
and stand close to my God,
in my cabin built of logs and mud,
and roof that's built of sod.

August 1962

At this writing I had returned to FAA from twelve years' absence. The airman's world had beckoned again, and I found myself retraining for the unique role we grounded ones play in the drama of flight. This familiarization trip was part of that training.

"Fam-Trips" Are Worthwhile

"Fairchild 98, can you get by the DC-6 ahead of you?"

"That's affirmative, we can get by."

"Fairchild 98, taxi into position——Fairchild 98, cleared for take-off; contact Departure Control on 119.1."

Captain Ken Wilkings, Co-pilot Gene Stolz, and Flight Engineer Tim Jackson turned wheels, snapped switches, pushed levers, read dials and called signals, and a heavy truck became a living thing, stepping lightly and confidently into the morning sky. She carried cargo for a "far-away place with a strange sounding name."

Two FAA students, Margaret Brown and Dean Nichols, tucked away into the corners of the flight deck, were awed observers on a "fam-trip" to Nome, Alaska. The flight would take us northwest along Victor Airway 440 at 8500 feet through mountains rising higher on either side, over plains and tundra and rolling hills and frozen rivers, and, toward the end, across 150 miles of frozen sea.

The few clouds were breaking up, and as the C-123 climbed out at near cruising speed of 140 knots, famed Mount McKinley and Mount Foraker stood out like beacons 135 miles to the north. So Captain Wilkings called Air Traffic Control and canceled his IFR Flight Plan, requesting VFR Ontop.

Thirty minutes out, a grand old lady, the DC-6 we had taxied around, passed us, climbing. But as she passed, she was level with us and seemed only yards away. There is something wonderful about an airplane in flight as seen from an airplane in flight. Relative motions are little or none, and the wonder of flight is experienced for the miracle that it is.

But ahead were mountains.

The Alaska Range, standing up out of the low scattered mist and spread with the bright morning sun, looked hard, even brittle, and very, very cold. Even the shadows cast by the ridges were sharp and black in contrast to the soft white glare of the mountains. Off to the north the Cathedral Mountains stood with brown stony walls so steep that neither ice nor snow could cling to them before the clawing winds.

A few months back I had crossed these same mountains in a Hercules on her way to Galena and Kotzebue. But she cruised at 21,000 feet and 260 knots; so the mountains were just a relief map spread out below. This time, at 8500 feet, there was an intimacy with the ragged peaks that was both terrible and beautiful.

For eighteen years I have known much about Rainy and Ptarmigan passes, but I have never flown through them. Perhaps I never will. But today, in the clear and still air, I was the student standing touching-close to the Master Painter as He brushed each ragged rock, each steep-walled valley into place. Vivid in my mind now is the long but low and easy route of Ptarmigan Pass, the short but narrow Rainy Pass with its distinctive "dogleg," and the several inviting yet false pass entrances.

The village of Farewell is not in the mountains.

Surely the charts show that clearly—now; but it took seeing from the sky to set this unlikely place in order in our minds. And who could ever forget Little Egypt Mountain, standing alone and marking the western entrance to Rainy Pass?

I don't know where I would have built McGrath; and I admit that the view from the air matched the pictures I had seen. But from our comfortable seat, riding on the soft ribbon of the wind, McGrath seemed out of context. As Captain Wilkings said, looking out across the frozen land, "Just miles and miles of nothing but miles and miles." We almost had to accept by faith that on those rolling hills, and in those hollows and waters and over those broad plains, is much life.

Around eleven-thirty we crossed the Golden Yukon, white, frozen, and still; and again, standing close to the Master Painter, we could see why she took her curious, skirting, final approach to the sea; there were low mountains in the way.

Fifteen minutes later came Unalakleet and Norton Sound. But the ocean was now a frozen lake; there were no breakers on the beaches, no moving water, no sound. As at McGrath, the operator at Unalakleet (actually, remoted from Nome) confidently took our position report and gave us the Nome weather —temperature minus 23 degrees, but with a bright sun and calm wind. With below zero and a sharp wind and a chill factor of some minus 75 degrees at Unalakleet, the flight crew elected to overfly the station this trip and get the few pounds we had for them back perhaps on a bush flight. I didn't know the details surrounding the decision; but it seemed a wise one.

I wasn't frightened or even anxious as we paddled out over the sea, sometimes as much as twenty miles from shore; but I was poignantly aware of our very lives depending on the faithfulness of both of those supposedly soulless engines and also of the unknown men who maintained them.

We reported our position over Cape Nome, and I recalled that I had heard of it—once. I also realized, now, that I would never forget it.

And then the traffic jam at Nome Airport. At Nome? There are two places in the world that come to most people's minds when they think of the "ends of the earth," Timbuktu and Nome, Alaska.

As we listened on our monitoring earphones to the Nome operator professionally giving his airport advisories, we realized there were two bush flights landing, a light plane waiting for takeoff, a C-123 twenty miles south landing runway 09 and a C-123 twenty miles east landing runway 27. We were the second C-123.

But the Air Force courteously did a 360 while Captain Wilkings slid his heavy bird onto the runway with not a bounce or jar of wheels. (He was aided a bit by the smooth ice on the runway.) The Air Force landed, the light plane took off, and calm returned to the Nome airport—although the word "returned" may give a wrong impression; calm seems to be the way of life in Nome.

Chief "Sputz" Roche and Journeymen John Bauers and Dick Sackett, Sr., let us drift quietly into their roomy and modern-looking station on the second floor and just look, for a while, out the large windows at a neat and orderly airport all black and white in the bright sunlight.

Introductions came casually, and questions were answered easily as Margaret asked about the station, its frequencies, about FAA housing, water supply, and more. It was interesting to find that, although Nome Flight Service Station has all the standard FSS frequencies, they were given a special one of 122.5 because the flat land and level ocean allowed transmissions on 122.2 from high-flying craft to splash over to Nome even though the planes themselves were near to and calling stations beyond the normal range of VHF. Nome is no longer a name on a map. The city, the FSS, and the men there are now real in our hearts and minds.

I cannot say the old cliché "The return trip was uneventful."

As we leveled out at our eastbound VFR altitude of 7500 feet, I noted quietly to myself that that would be 1000 feet closer to those jagged, reaching peaks of the Alaska Range than when we brushed them going over.

Around four we found ourselves north of Beaver Mountain and Bonanza Creek and saw the many valleys filled with gold-dredge tailings. Here was history engraved in stone. And the stories told over the intercom of the many planes that had vanished there made us look deeper into those valleys, hoping to catch a glimpse of the mystery that had claimed them.

Captain Stolz was flying left seat as we left Farewell and slipped the famous mountains again under our wings.

"When you are approaching Rainy Pass from this side," he spoke into our earphones, "*don't* take that first left turn; it's a dead-end trap. Take the second, right there. And see that dogleg? It's left, then sharp right again." We saw and understood.

The weather had been clear, calm and beautiful all the way until Hayes River on our return; but by then the sun was down, and a soft white undercast spread eastward below us. Beginning promptly at five, the ash from Saint Augustine and the sun below the horizon teamed up to give us a fantastic sunset, almost as though the volcano herself were lighting the night sky with fire from the deep.

Sixteen miles out of Anchorage the undercast conveniently faded away, the night closed in, and the lights of Anchorage spread out invitingly in the distance ahead.

A light northerly crosswind kept Captain Stolz busy holding his iron bird in line with runway 6 right; but when touchdown came, and the winged thing became again what she really was, a truck on wheels, the transition was as gentle and smooth as a beautiful woman placing her favorite jewel on a cloth of velvet.

The glorious sunset, the closing night, the welcoming expanse of the city lights, and the perfect landing surely placed the final brushstrokes on the canvas of a perfect day.

"Fam-trips" are worthwhile.

ANC FSS
February 12, 1976

This probably should have been in my book, *Islands of Experience*, but it didn't get there. So I include it here because it certainly is a very important sketch of a very memorable period of my life, the summer of 1965.

I loved the people of Cordova.

From a Letter to My Mother

. . . It doesn't seem that I have given you much of an account of an unusual summer's experience; and, being a little rummy this dark Sunday afternoon, I'm not so sure that I can ramble through one without it being rather dull; but here goes.

You asked about my use of the term "ship." I'm not sure where the dividing line lies between a boat and a ship unless it is somewhere within the emotional heart of the speaker or writer. Certainly, the M/V *Brant*, my thirty-two-foot fiberglass gilnetter, was all I had between life and death while facing the open and often angry sea; and I cannot conceive of any mere "boat" standing up so bravely and competently to those thundering and impatient waters; and so she became my little "ship."

Some outfit in Seattle built around a hundred of them a few years back for use primarily as gilnetters up in Bristol Bay where it is also often quite rough; and the Alaska Dept. of Fish and Game bought several for use as patrol boats. In her all white with black trim she is a beautiful craft with a full, wave-defying bow and plenty of freeboard, and looks very much like what she is, a haughty and confident police boat.

I didn't realize when I took the job that I was to be (besides a boat skipper) a Protection Officer (game warden); but the first thing I knew I had a uniform, shoulder patch, and badge.

I had so much to learn that the first few months were more of a dizzy whirl than the romantic adventure I had expected; but even so, memory and recollection fill in more fully all the time, the awareness of the romance and adventure that was really there. My "beat" stretched from the western end of Prince William Sound to Cape Suckling or Kayak Island, a distance of about 180 miles and 10 to 50 miles wide; a total area of roughly 4000 to 6000 square miles. Of course I didn't

31

touch every bay, fjord, cove, and lagoon; I couldn't in six short months; but I certainly became well acquainted with a beautiful, fascinating, and impressive area of Alaska.

We have been back in the city for nearly three months now; and as we delve back into the summer's (now brief) experience, we see that the greatest part of the experience, or maybe the real fullness of the experience itself, was the close contact with the people.

People and personality are such nebulous things that it seems almost impertinent to even attempt to describe them, and yet somehow we must.

Although there are, of course, people of all social levels, educational levels and financial and moral levels, even in Cordova, the "they" will generally mean the majority, the hard-fishing, hard-drinking, easy-living, and frequently deep-thinking fishermen and their wives.

In my most brief observation I concluded, very roughly, that 1 to 2 percent were outright fish pirates and would steal fish from behind the markers, during a closed period, or by use of illegal methods or gear any time there was the slightest chance of getting away with it. The next 8 percent would do the same, in degree varying from the above to only if they were very, very sure that not even another fisherman would catch them. The remaining 90 percent, I felt, were sincere and honest fishermen without whose cooperation we could never have protected the fishery from excessive, and thus destructive, harvesting. As you, of course, realize, unless the minimum number of spawning salmon get up the streams, the runs will continually diminish until this bountiful and generous, God-given, and most delicious food supply is gone.

My last trip out with the *Brant* was a three-weeks' stay down at Bering River, near the abandoned Indian village of Katalla, during the late silver salmon run. I was the only Fish and Game representative there and had to cover two areas about ten miles apart. This required crossing the bar out into the ocean to get from one area to the other. The fishing period was for half of

32

the week only so that during the closed half we had quite a bit of time to huddle together in the anchorages and drink coffee and tell each other lies and counter lies and for me to hear all that was wrong with the Fish and Game, or "that ———," Ralph Pirtle, or "that --- of-a ---" Ray Baxter, or "that (dirtier name yet)," Bob Anderson, my boss, or, in other words, to find myself in a corner taking on all comers and defending the Fish and Game and its purposes, methods and aims. (The above-named men are really fine and highly respected fellows. I'm merely quoting a few disgruntled fishermen.) It was generally in a spirit of serious though good humor, and no one ever got really insulting with me; but there were times when I noticed a definite weariness; and I had to return to my own little ship and rest.

Still, the get-togethers weren't all sparring with me, and the most interesting and revealing times were when I could just sit there in the tiny cabin of a fish boat (barely 8 by 10 feet, which included a stove, sink, two or more bunks, table, toilet, all their food supplies, books, magazines, cameras, etc., and six to ten people) drinking coffee (I never drank liquor on the job, and the fishermen genuinely respected that) and listen to their banter and occasionally surprisingly deep insight into life and philosophy.

At first observation, they appeared to be a drunken and immoral lot, with values not much beyond their boats and gear and the fish and a bottle or the bar. And yet, in the way, not so much in what they did, but in the way in which they approached the baser functions of man they seemed to free those functions and foul language of any stigma of filth or degradation. As a result, though they frequently broke the so-called normal rules of a so-called normal society, I could not feel that they were nearly as sinful as, again, the so-called upper echelons of society when they break those same rules.

I do not mean to suggest in any way that society in general should relax its rules, but simply to say that by living so closely to a people who lived so openly I could perceive that rules in themselves are really meaningless; that it is really the spirit with which they are lived or ignored that has any meaning or meat to it at all.

Well, this is hardly a thorough dissertation on the fishermen of Prince William Sound; but it should give you at least a glimpse of the rich and revealing experiences both June, in her work in the cannery, and I on my tiny ship, found this summer. If you didn't receive any of the earlier-mentioned essays or poems, be sure to let me know, and I'll send you copies which will fill in in much more poignant expression, the imprint of the geography, weather, and people on me. . . .

January 23, 1966

Our Own

The fog hangs low and drifting, drifting swiftly on the
 breeze;
the sky peeks through and spreads its blue for a moment
 on the sea.
The wavelets ring their tinkling bells against the hull;
and from the sky comes the hungry cry of a lonely,
 gliding gull.

. . . . . .

Two pursers hang on slanting scopes of anchor line.
The cluster of small boats attached speaks well of wine,
but friendship too and sharing of tall tales
of bigger hauls and thicker fogs and gales.

. . . . . .

The flooding tide so soon will hide the sand surrounding
 us,
and then will be but a tiny sea with a wall of mist, and thus
three tiny ships will find themselves at anchor and all
 alone,
in a world that I, with the mist and the sky and solitude,
 call our own.

Aboard the M/V Brant
Kanak Island, Alaska
September 9, 1965

35

Cordova Boat Harbor

It's raining. Some people tell me that to say "It's raining," or to say "Cordova, Alaska," is to say the same thing.

Well, it does rain in Cordova; but the sun shines too. And even when it doesn't shine from the sky, it "shines from the hearts of its people." I think the names they have given their boats will reveal this.

Some time ago I walked every float in another boat harbor; and as I read the names on the boats I was stirred with a feeling difficult to describe. It was much like the experience of having to listen to someone do a poor job of telling a not really funny story.

How refreshing to walk the floats in Cordova's boat harbor and see imagination, romance, adventure, and sometimes even audacity reflected there. There was a sober respect for an unforgiving sea that has swept so many of her men, and some of her women, into eternity; there was also a gentle, good-natured love for the water that gives these people their economic life and, I suppose, a measure of their spiritual life as well.

Oh, I know that in Cordova there are honest and some fairly honest businessmen and women, that there are drunks who believe that all life comes from a bottle; and there are total abstainers who think that life comes from piety and church attendance and a display of righteousness. I know that there are girls who have lost their virginity reluctantly, and others who have lost it on purpose; and there are those who, because they had parents who knew how to love them, learned early in life to put out their stabilizers whenever a storm approached; and so they grew up to be truly beautiful women. And I know there are real Christians in Cordova who have acknowledged Jesus as very truly the Christ and have accepted Him as Savior, as have I.

But this story is not about any of these. This is about boats and the uniqueness of their names, and what those names reveal about those who named them—and maybe just a little about a few of the people some of the names bring to mind.

Listen to the names on some of the pursers, crab boats, and larger gillnetters: *Vecci, Marci J., Scotty, Kukak, Min O Taur* (there was a big-tired trail bike lashed down over the hatch), *Shannon, Norel* (She was steel and had that hard look that steel boats have; the name seemed to fit, though I don't know why), *Hayjo, Stork, Voyageur, Aunt Martha* (maybe she paid for the boat; but I'd rather believe someone loved her).

There was *Lady Brenda, Dawn L., Tri-K, Combo, Tamnik, Dragnet, Midnight Ryder, Mystic, Towhee, U & I, Kathleen L., Krissel, Styx* (a most unusual name for a boat), *Demetra M., Dickie Bird, Sea Fever, Kingfisher* (the names weren't always original, but they showed a poetic awareness of the sea), *Blue Fox, Frantic* (well, things get pretty frantic just before the season opens, during the season many times, and just before it closes; and even sometimes during the long, quiet winters when the bills run high and the money runs low, and the season is months away).

There was *Shamrock* (yes, she was green and sort of looked like an Irishman, though I couldn't tell you, really, what an Irishman looks like), and there was *Cindy.* (We used to have a beloved dog named Cindy, which reminds me of Cordova dogs: they multiply; but like the gentle, friendly though independent old rascal that followed me around the floats today, I've never known one to be mean.)

There was *Diamond Lil, Wm. Lee, Channel Cat, Pay Day, Marauder, Icy Cape* (a name and a beautiful purse seiner that both reflect the character of the owner, Les Maxwell; he and his brother Bob, whatever they may be to anyone else, were real men, real seamen, and real gentlemen to me.

(During the summer of 1965 I operated the M/V *Brant* as Protection/Boat Officer for the Alaska Department of Fish and Game. I was a seagoing cop, yet these men, like so many other Cordova fishermen, showed kindness and consideration for my struggling efforts at learning the job at hand; and still they showed me respect for the authority they knew I would exercise over them, or any others, if the situation called for it.

(It was the people, mostly, who helped establish a bond that

37

year that I shall never be able to sever; partly because I don't want to, I suppose. But though it is an elastic bond, it is an indestructible one.)

But back to names: There was *Patty S, Pammy C, Glacier Queen, John Jason, Miss Lynn, Sue B.* (She is a lovely little double-ender—I have an old nostalgic love for double-enders—with a black, wooden hull. I remember nine years ago watching her owner carefully, patiently, and with remarkable craftsmanship repair her afterdeck back where the sides came together on her pointed stern. Each piece must have had several angles, yet when I looked at them today they were still fitted together as neatly and firmly as they were nine years ago.)

And there was also *O. Nerka* (another little double-ender), *Arctic Tern, Tammy J* (she looked like a yacht, and I don't mean a cheap, playboy yacht), *Linda Lee, Northwind, Tina, Islander, Stardust, Cheerful II* (she looked it—lots of free-board and bow flare, high gunnels), *Rainbow, Pacific Warrior* (with a very forward-thrusting bow and wide flare she looked like a warrior, but not mean, just ready). *Jenel.* (My cousin, owner of Nichols Boat Works down in the States, built her ten or twelve years ago. She appeared to be still in fine shape, but she was for sale. Strangely, it made me a little sad.)

Still more, there was *Lena C, Brad-Lee, Darlin, Tomboy, Nina-Fay, Franz Joseph.* (She was old and wooden and had that reverse curve to her wooden bowstem so typical of the exciting sailing ships of history. In spite of her age and the obvious effects of time and storm, she sat there quiet and proud like a crusty old skipper who still knows he is a match for the sea.) Also *Chum, Raimi, Amy, Sylvia Ann, Rustler, Junior, Nadine, Ne-Ow* (not misspelled), *Malano, Buddy, Gail, Due North, Karen Mae, Catalina* (of Cordova, too), *Roald, Sea Ranger, Waif, H&H, Siren, Ms. Natural, Dungeness, Mary Lou, Prosperity, Gypsy Queen,* and *John David.*

(I'd like to say that this last one was named after a beloved old friend, John David Solf. She wasn't. She was named after another fine young man. But if he will allow me, I'd like to tell a little about John David Solf. He was different, not in the way we often use the word when applying it to characters, but he just wasn't like ordinary people. Yet there was a magnetic warmth about him that few could resist. If he wore a left black and a right green hip boot, it was simply for the practical reason that the right black and left green ones leaked. He was a highly capable and really dedicated Department of Fish and Game biologist. He lost his life less than a year ago while on a research project out on Prince William Sound. Some ice gave way and dropped him into the merciless, frigid water. He was rescued just before he died, but the numbing cold had taken him past the point of no return. Few would have thought of calling him John or David. He was always John David; and the beauty and integrity of this large, ocean-going crab boat named *John David* would certainly do honor to a mighty fine man.)

Comet and *Packer* were two of the power barges there. These ugly ducklings of the boating world will never grow up to be swans; but they have a beauty not seen with the eyes. Rugged, square, shallow-draft, plodding workhorses, they do the large-volume hauling that leaves the nimble-footed ones free to be. *Comet* is owned and operated by Bobbie Anderson, a blood son of Cordova and the fishing world. In 1965 he was the Protection Officer for the Department of Fish and Game. Though gentle and good-natured with a delightful sense of humor, he had the cool and quiet determination to carry out the task of enforcement. There were a few who hated him, and one, I know, who wrote some nasty words about him on the inside of the Cordova jail door. When Bobbie learned about it, he very typically burst out laughing. I couldn't imagine hating Bobbie Anderson myself. But then, he never caught me illegally fishing either.

Most of the cabin skiffs were not named, just a Coast Guard number; but a few were, and it seems to me that their names say something nebulously, but definitely, different from their bigger sisters. Listen to them.

Quinnat, Opna Havat, Shar-Mor, Osprey, Tate, Baby Doll, Quickie, Misdeal, Umma, Shirtail, Scrappy, Linda K, Red Baron, King James, Muggsy, Black Oak, Hopeless. (It was definitely not a hopeless future captain who named this tiny seed of a ship. Rather, the name reflects an infectious sense of humor he inherited from his father. But having just a bit of fatherly interest in him myself, I would suggest a better name might be something like *Learnin' Fast, Hello Future,* or *On My Way.*) *Tyron* is such a beautiful name it almost seems it should have been on a purser; but she is a well-kept, seaworthy little skiff. Maybe her skipper will one day put that name on his dream ship.

And last is the exceptionally well-designed Alaska Department of Fish and Game M/V *Montague,* skippered by able and experienced Captain Harry Curran. Captain Harry is not a large man, but his stature stands tall among those who know him and the sea. He has an incredible capacity for work; and his ship is kept so spotless that the worn cliché "You could eat off his engine-room floor," is literally true.

When I first met Captain Harry in 1965, he took me on a familiarization trip out over the Copper Sands aboard the old power barge, *Shad.* At a certain moment I started to whistle softly. He curtly (unusual for him) ordered me not to whistle in the wheelhouse: "You'll whistle up a storm." Now I'm not calling that superstition. There are a lot of strange things that happen in this brief life. Anyway, I never whistled in his wheelhouse again.

Some years later I was running a sixty-foot LCM that had been converted by lengthening it out ten feet and by building on a high steel cover over the well-deck, making a roomy cabin for hauling crews. But this made her skate in a wind like a sailboat without a centerboard or keel. One day we were running light from the Anchorage Port dock to a derrick barge a mile or so out when I thought of Captain Harry. I asked my deckhand if he'd ever heard of whistling up a storm. Having never worked on the water before, he hadn't. Well, the wind rarely blows in Anchorage, really blows I mean, so I said, "Shall we try it?" He was game, and besides, he had as much curiosity as I did, so he said, "Sure," and I started whistling.

In the ten previous days we'd had hardly a ripple, and on this day it was nearly flat calm; but in less than ten minutes we were fighting the gosh-awfulest wind storm I've seen in the Anchorage area. Well, I quit whistling, of course, and the wind went down; but it seems a shame, Captain Harry—I do like to whistle at my work.

But coming back to Cordova, I'd like to end with a curious observation. I believe the Cordova fishermen love their women more than most other men do. It could be that the year I spent with them in 1965 let me see deeper into their characters than most observers are privileged to do. But as I read all those girls' and women's names, so carefully painted on bow after bow, I read something more than just some female names. I read respect, and affection, and friendship, and, of course, real love.

Oh, I suppose there are a lot of people who could tell me a lot of bad things about the Cordova fishermen; but I don't think I'd listen. I'd just rather walk their harbor floats and read the names of those beautiful, floating things that tell the secret story of their lives.

October 1974

Wrangell Narrows

Way back and once upon some geologic time, the mountains parted, just a little bit; the sea rushed in, and Wrangell Narrows was born. The impossible, incongruous fact was here: the sea among the mountaintops. But the sea is made for ships.

Mountain climbers, a strange and daring breed, know the intense concentration, the singleness of purpose it would take, even using pitons, rope, skill, experience and total confidence, to scale famed Mt. McKinley's Wickersham Wall.

The other night, from 1:00 to 3:00 A.M., three men with intense concentration and singleness of purpose used compass, rudder, engines, and experience with the same skill and total confidence to slip this namesake ship, 5,000 tons of it, through this narrow slot in the unforgiving stony mountains.

Beauty has many names: a rose, a sunset, a woman; but beauty can be performance too; and what I saw was beautiful.

In either case, whether hanging by some strand of nylon line thousands of feet above the sea, or guiding this massive ship along this narrow slot upon the sea, the mountains are terribly unforgiving of any carelessness, incapacity or neglect, mercilessly unforgiving; but the opposite—the skilled, precise, successful performance—is excellence, and excellence is sheer beauty. Like God, the mountains tell us, "Show me the utmost in respect, obey precisely my laws, and you will be worthy of the rewards I give." We obey, and the rocks reward us with safe and quiet passage, protected from the angry ocean outside.

The fame of the Inside Passage, and especially of Wrangell Narrows, is world known; but like so many things of unbelievable beauty, the human spirit cannot fully accept and believe until it has shared an experience. But here was even more than the now believable beauty of ageless mountains towering over an ocean-going ship; here too I experienced the now believable beauty of excellence.

And during the darkest hours of the night, the quiet crew of the Motorship *Wickersham* completed the safe passage of Wrangell Narrows.

Aboard the M/S Wickersham
March 21, 1969

So You Wrote a Book—Why?

Alaska is that magic word that still, after sixteen years, thrills me as the cry "Gold, gold!" must have thrilled the early Cheechahkos who later became Sourdoughs by enduring her challenges and claiming her promises. As surely as Alaska spawns her salmon, she "spawned" my first book, *Islands of Experience*—but how? I, who live by words, find myself struggling, groping for the words that will answer that question.

I believe that all of us are bound to express our innermost being, that it is absolutely essential, and that we *will* express it.

The most obvious forms of expression are the arts: painting, music, dance, design; but I have seen this expression in work as well. I have seen men operating purse seiners with the joy of creativity; and one could detect the graceful and expressive motions of ballet in the artful handling of net and wheel and power.

But my compulsion is words. When an experience wells up inside of me, it must burst forth in words. I think I can tell it best in the beginning words of one of the first poems in my book. My wife paints and can find in the artist's tools of canvas and oils a form of escape, or relief, or rest. I had been running up tight for a spell, so she talked me into trying her tools, even if I didn't come up with a masterpiece. Secretly I had always thought I could paint mountains (you know, if I *really* tried), so I agreed to try. She left the room.

I picked up the brush, looked out at Alaska's magnificent Chugach Mountains just starting to reflect the glory of a setting sun, and started to draw. I drew three lines each curving into the next. They looked like the three I drew in the third or fourth grade entitled "Hills." For some time I struggled with that terrible frustration of *knowing* what I wanted to express and being helpless to express it. Finally I laid the brush down, sat down on the daveno and wrote: "Painting: You take the brush and place the oils on canvas there, / and let me play with words. / Paint mountains high, you dare, / but is it really fair / to thrust the brush into my hand? / My medium is words, and rather with my pen / I'd paint the frozen land. . . ."

But Alaska had her hand in mine almost from the start of

our love affair. Nearly fourteen years ago, filled with the spirit of Alaska, I looked on one of my wife's paintings, a spectacular, rugged mountain scene, and wrote "The Glacier Priest": "Across the frigid waters stands / the lonely Glacier Priest; / his sermon never-ending as you stand alone and feast / your eyes upon this monument of God's creation plan / of tall, eternal mountain that is part of mortal man. / Your ears may strain to listen to the voice of which I speak / and hear no sound but the wind around / each tall and lonely peak. / So listen with your eyes, my friend, / and think on Him above / and let the mountain tell your heart of the vastness of His love. . . ."

There are words and phrases that have been used to describe Alaska for so long that they are almost clichés; but like those three simple words, "I love you," there are no better words. In the poem "I Love You," are the lines: "yet have you ever seen a sunrise, burst forth in colors all aglow and said, 'It is the same, it is not new'?"

That's the way it is with Alaska's words like "vastness," "endless reaches," "mountains rising ageless from the sea," "silence."

Oh, I could tell you of another great love, Prince William Sound, and a summer working her "vast and endless reaches" as Protection/Boat Officer for the Alaska Department of Fish and Game; and I could tell you of poems like "Prince William Sound, Alaska" or essays like "My Beloved Family," which were spawned there; but I'd better end for now with this story.

My son, a truly beautiful person and to whom *Islands of Experience* is dedicated, died when the tugboat he was on sank off Anchor Point near Homer, Alaska, in November, 1966. But while he lived, he shared with that extra gift of sharing that the "too few" have.

It was late in August of 1961. Lloyd and I had gone on a two-week caribou-hunting trip up in the high country about 180 miles northeast of Anchorage. Going as far as we could by car, we loaded up our boat and headed north for forty miles across Lake Louise, Lake Susitna, Lake Tyone and north down the Tyone River. We made camp that night in a tiny clearing near the foot of Mt. Tyone. Mt. Tyone (a beautiful name, isn't it) rises not over 1,500 feet above the land, but since it is the only prominence for some miles north and for many miles east, south or west, it presented a challenge we couldn't resist. There were plenty of caribou down on the broad tundra for easy pack back to camp; but "the mountain was there." After a few days and a couple of caribou, we looked at the mountain. I don't know who first challenged the other, but such was sharing with Lloyd that it was probably only the voice of the wilderness saying, "Climb." I'm sure we just looked at each other and said, "Let's go."

Blueberries were everywhere, fall was in the air, and that air was clean, and crisp, and pure. Somewhere up the side of that mountain Lloyd looked back once and saw me sitting down to write; so he just patiently and lovingly stopped, climbed upon a boulder and started looking with those incredible, eaglelike eyes of his. When I had finished writing (on the back of a bloodstained map packet) he came back and, with a gentle smile of approval, read: "As I climb steadily higher up the side of this mountain, and the wild country falls away beneath, I think, 'Ah Wilderness, whose crown is your mountain, whose glory is your color, and whose soul is your silence.' And that's the thing about the silence in Alaska; it is so deep, so enormous one can hear it even above, or better, through the sound of the city, the rush of wind through the trees, or the tumbling voice of a waterfall—

"And then we reach the top, and my gaze travels outward from my feet and falls over a hundred lakes in any direction and all backed by endless, snow-clad mountains. A thousand square miles and, right now, all mine.

"Here on this mountaintop where time and distance too are mine, and the silence is everywhere, I can know at least something of the glory of God; for it must have taken great joy to create even such as this."

I had to write those words.

That is why I "wrote" the book. They were islands of experience that demanded expression.

March 1974

45

LLOYD'S POND

Boggie Dingles
Lloyd's Pond
Alaska, 1966

My newest son and my beloved Jo,

A moment past it was the first but now the second of July. The sky is cast with clouds, and raindrops now and then tap gently on the roof. And yet, the light from brilliant sun just o'er the Pole sends filtered glow all 'round our mirrored pond, so I can see the grasses wave on yonder shore.

The hiss of my gas lantern, resting here upon a blazo box, has drowned out the rush of breeze as it caresses all the trees, but still, I see them sway and hear them say they love me as they know I love each one.

I sit alone, except for Cindy, our old hound, here by my side. I came up here three days before to finish up the chore of insulation and the paneling that make this wooden box a place against the storm; a cabin warm that, raised of my own hands, now folds its wooden walls around me in their thanks for my creating them.

I realize with just a bit of guilt—well, quite a bit—how long it's been since I have written you. The passing days of work and solitude, the fresh creative bath of nature all around, have blown away the fog of city life and set me free so I can see the magic pattern of the life around and set the patterned phrases down and thus record, for my posterity at least, the thoughts of one who wonders 'bout such things as love and life and, of them both, their mystery.

And so I put them down. And as I polished up the edges and regrouped a phrase, as each new thought came tumbling in to match the one before, as in "My Cabin Door," I couldn't keep away the picture of our Denny and our Jo. For this I know, however crude and bungling is my prose, however singsong or beyond the ken of men my poems are, you two can read them and find deep therein some beauty, or some wisdom, or some thought profound; the latter quite a compliment, I've found.

Of course, the "poem" (quite a stretch of definition I'm afraid) is nothing special, as you see; but still, it pleases me, because it paints a picture of a part of this small cabin that I love, a bit more special even than the roof above or walls so warm and strong or even floor on which an army tank could rest with ease.

I guess I've rattled on enough for this wee hour. The dawn is sifting through the trees, and birds are tuning up their morning song; and sleep, that blest necessity, calls from my waiting bed.

Goodnight dear ones, 'nuf said,

DAD

My Cabin Door

A simple wooden door, made out of spruce, in fact,
and I can here assure you it is more than tacked.
For it is nailed one thousand times, it seems.
The night 'twas done I nailed them all again in dreams.

The outside boards from local trees were sawn,
their color creamy tan—well, like a fawn.
The grain is course and rough. No Sitka spruce were
   these.
Susitna Valley land produced these trees.

The layer next is set at forty-five degrees
to give it strength and warmth more than to please.
But still, it pleases me. I know each piece that's there;
for that's the story here: of love and care.

The inside layer is a joy to gaze upon.
From Sitka spruce these lovely pieces sawn.
Fine-textured is the artist's word for such a wood.
I matched them up together best I could.

The handles are a piece of sturdy one-by-four.
No question here whereon to grasp the door.
And in their strength a comfort deep is felt and known,
secure and warm e'en when I'm here alone.

But oh, those hinges—massive, black, and rusty things;
I wouldn't trade them for the golden ones of kings.
Scrounged from abandoned mine or some mysterious
   place,
they add the perfect final touch upon the face

Of this, my simple, lovely, wooden cabin door;
but then I've told you all of this before.
But what I haven't said, and what is really there,
is evidence of work and love and care.

June 30, 1966

48

Lloyd's Pond

"Faraway places with strange-sounding names." And where am I right now? I am sitting in a silent cabin on a five-acre piece we call Boggie Dingles, on the shore of Lloyd's Pond, Alaska. Soon I will cast off from our dock, ghost down to the tiny channel, across the east end of Mirror Lake, through the larger channel with its towering walls of golden birch, properly punctuated with dark-green spruce, and out into Big Lake.

If the northwest breeze holds, we, the *Sea of Galilee* and I, will spend the next four or five hours sailing the south shore, silently riding on the soft ribbon of the wind, past dozens and dozens of cabins and even some fine homes. Rarely will I see a living soul. This is Tuesday; and the citizens of Anchorage are in the city earning the money to pay for the luxury of a cabin in the wilderness. Curious, isn't it, that a cabin could now be termed a luxury, so much are they a part of or an extension of the city, and home.

Still, when I look away with the telescope of my mind and see the turmoil and the terror, the war and fear and hunger, the twisted and empty lives, the struggling—man against man and people against people; and then I zoom the lens back to here and now and look out my window onto a peaceful pond all lovingly wrapped in the green, the green-gold, and the gold of late September, I realize that, for a little while, I am blessed to be in the very heart of that "Far away place with the strange-sounding name."

Some would call this Heaven. But I think Heaven will be ever more glorious and peaceful even than this. For now, I'll just call it "Lloyd's Pond."

Lloyd's Pond, Alaska
September 26, 1978

The Voice

I thought I heard the fall wind talk to me today.
Its whispering invitation seemed to say
that I should stay
and watch the falling, golden leaves
turn to snowflakes white;
and wait, as Indian summer days
lose their thin, protective sunlight rays
and turn to winter's silent, gentle night.

Oh, peace and stillness,
worn and calloused concepts though they be,
still hold for me
the healing channel through which God can give;
and I receive,
knowing that through Him,
I live.

In truth,
the voice of God was riding on the autumn wind today,
and saying, "Yes, you can both go and stay.
For with the mind I gave you, though you go,
you can return at will, and hear my voice,
ever calling on the autumn wind.

"But as you go, my son, remember that, to hear my voice,
you must, at least in heart,
drop down upon your knees and pray. And then
the healing peace is yours,"
He told me, on the autumn wind today.

Lloyd's Pond, Alaska
September 29, 1978

A Day of Sacrifice

Today we sacrificed a tree—and we cried.

Twenty feet behind our cabin a huge birch with perfect branches all filled with gold stood in joyous splendor, leaning slightly toward the cabin as if both in protection and adoration.

We knew it had to come down under controlled conditions, because if we waited, it was only time away till it would fall, crushing the roof of the cabin. A storm would come some dark night when the earth was wet and soft, and the shallow roots would lose their hold; and its own weight, and the nudge of the wind, would bring it down on the little house it so clearly loved.

So we carefully made the undercut, aiming it less than eight feet from the northwest corner, made the back cut and watched it drop swiftly onto the bed we had prepared. It never complained or even looked at us with pleading eyes.

For well over 100 years it had been growing there, enduring winters harsh and cold and budding forth each spring with the soft and lovely green, and then each fall filling an ever-increasing space with its glorious gold, just practicing for the days when we would come and love it for the beauty that it shared.

Killing this lovely thing was not an easy decision; sometimes the altar of practicality can be so ugly. But we knew it had to be done; and we knew we would cry. As we looked at her there, glorious, glorious even in death, we cried; and in spoken prayer, we thanked God that we could cry. Oh, how empty, how hollow life must be for those who cannot cry.

We felled a few more trees, cut them into wood . . . had some lunch, and then I left with the sailboat. . . . Brisk broad reach all the way to the sailing club where the A-7.0 was just finishing repairing his rudder. We sailed together, sort of playing tag, for an hour or two down along the south shore, and then headed back. At Burnt Point we parted; they to the sailing club, and I home. . . . We had another excellent supper, relived our day, and read another chapter in our book.

This has been a different day; but then, a day of sacrifice cannot be like an ordinary day.

Lloyd's Pond, Alaska
September 22, 1978

JO ANN

The poems and essay in this section were written a number of years ago by my daughter, Jo Ann (Nichols) Harris, when she was a seventeen-year-old girl. That is what gives them their refreshing, youthful quality.

Uncertainty

I'm standing still, but life is rushing by;
it's like a stream, and I'm still on the shore.
I'm young; I've many years before I die;
I am alive but do not know what for.

What do I want from life—what can I give?
Where do I fit in life's complex design?
Where do I stand? I know not why I live.
What shall I do with this one life of mine?

In youth, alone, confused, I only know
that I must find the answer on my own.
If ever I'm to reap, I first must sow
a seed in soil still to me unknown.

I must decide myself what is to be;
for no one else can live this life for me.

November 1961

A Poetry of Seasons

Spring

I feel joy, for I see the sun.
I feel young, for I know it is spring.
Each day the air grows warm,
the snow melts,
I walk in puddles.
I welcome spring.

Fall

I feel empty, for I see death.
I feel old, for things are dying.
The frost comes;
the trees are bare.
It is fall.

Summer

I feel like running.
The sun is hot.
I am alone and free and happy.
Nature is most alive in summer.
I am alive.
I love summer.

Winter

I feel peace, then awe.
Snow is pure;
the blizzard is terrible.
I feel cold,
then content by the fire.
Winter is black and white.

March 1962

Although my beloved daughter wrote the following, I still find it a difficult thing to accept that such a tender, loving person could lash out with such sharp-edged words. Still, I think you will agree with me that the undercurrent here is nevertheless one of tender compassion for a lost soul.

D. N.

Open Letter

(To a brilliant teacher but a cold intellectual)

Are you void of all tender emotions? Have you ever felt true compassion, patriotism, love of country, God, or nature? Sometimes I wonder if you have any self-love. It is necessary, you know, as well as self-respect.

Oh, but here—here is a feeling which you are capable of: you respect the mind. The educated mind does not tolerate these "soft" emotions, does it? Sex, yes, because sex is physical, biological, the mind can explain it. But love? I think not. The mind scorns it. The mind is too wise, too learned, much, much too intelligent to believe in such things. Love is an illusion in the minds of the less intelligent; and the mind is far above this.

Oh, I pity you in your blind intelligence—pity you because you cannot believe! Yes, you scorn my pity; you in your inimitable superiority, because you have the mind. Poor, wretched, hollow, empty man.

November 1961

And Now I Weep

How sad it is for me to see
so many people live
An aimless, pointless, fruitless life,
though they have much to give.

Their brains are more than average;
their looks are more than fair;
You'd think they'd count their blessings
and be more than glad to share.

But no, they can't be bothered
with the welfare of mankind.
The race is fast, they scramble on,
lest they be left behind.

*   *   *

They don't know what they're looking for—
happiness, I guess.
But only for themselves they search,
encased in selfishness.

The pleasures of the flesh, of drink,
of mere material things,
Are all they know of happiness;
and time speeds by on wings.

To think what they could give the world,
and to know them as they are,
Makes one cry out, "Wake up blind fool,
reach up, reach for a star!"

And now I weep, they do not hear.
O God, why did you put them here?
I guess it's not for man to ask,
to question God's design—
God made the man, He put him here;
perhaps, perhaps, he'll wake in time.

April 1962

Healing

The music swelled and filled my ear
with melody so sweet and clear
that for a while I was not here
but in a world untouched by fear;
and I worried not that war was near.

And then the music changed its pace;
and I was in a different place,
all dressed in silk and fancy lace—
no worries there of the power race.

Swelling now in swift crescendo,
the strings burst forth with soft, sweet sadness,
drifting from this world of madness
to one of melancholy gladness.

Oh, sweet music,
gently do you chase away
the cares and worries of the day,
and fill the body, mind, and soul
with strength to help us find the way
to meet with faith the coming day.

October 1961

ALMA JUNE

Twenty

Merrill Field
Anchorage, Alaska
March 30, 1960

My beloved wife,

At exactly 5:57 A.M. the brilliant sun in a northern sky came bursting over the ragged crest of the Chugach Mountains. Not an unusual phenomenon this, to the average mortal. But to me it was a moment, a mark in the endless ocean of time; for at that moment a period ended, to live on only in the memory of man.

For you and me that period, and those memories, were twenty years, one-fifth of a century together. Twenty years sharing the bright and the dark, sorrows and joys, success and failure, accomplishments and defeats, but most of all sharing the preparation for what really happened at that precise instant.

For, as the sun gained its ages-old yet ever new victory over the mountains to the east, a new day began, and if a new day then a new period, a new life for you and me.

Like the sunset, dimming is the past;
but like the sunrise, brighter, clearer
shows the road ahead.

No telling now if future bright or dark,
if sorrows to be felt or joy full-lived,
success to rise upon or failures faced,
accomplishment be ours,
or defeat known.

But one thing sure;
for twenty years two trees have grown,
their roots grown deep in earth,
and side by side,
their branches so entwined, that strength is known,
that neither could achieve alone.

So let the future roll,
its mysteries day by day unfold;
whatever be will all the better be, because,
this sunrise marked beginning, and an end,
but oh, a very special end
in time.

Love,
DEAN

To my wife, not on her birthday, not on our wedding day, not for Christmas or Valentine's Day or any other special day, but on this day because, on this day,

I Love You

I love you—
such simple words,
so aged and worn with time,
I wonder how I might repeat them here
in words that rhyme,
and have them still be new and fresh, alive,
and singing forth their news.

Still, roses grow year after year in sun and rain,
yet ever new and never one the same.
The sunrise comes day after day,
precisely ordered by celestial law,
yet have you ever seen a sunrise
burst forth, in colors all aglow,
and said, "It is the same, it is not new"?

And so it is with these three words,
so oft repeated time has ceased to count.
For when I say I love you,
I see the flowers of your heart arranged anew,
the sunrise of your face in fresh array
of colors that I never saw before.

And still, through all the change, the fresh, the new,
the constancy of love prevails,
like mountains rising ageless from the land,
or tides that rise forever from the sea.
And then I wonder, and I stop and look again,
and as I change my view,
I find,
the ever-same becomes the ever-new.

September 1963

59

The Circle

What happens
when I wrap my arms around you?
The circle thus completed
is as infinite
as time.

When we
who drift upon the void
see earth and home and life
and all we thought to be
the rod of iron
break up in pieces there
before our eyes,
then reach we must
for some security.

I know what happens
when I wrap my arms around you.
The circle thus completed
is as infinite as time.
Can there be
a more secure an anchor
than that which has
no end?

January 1972

To Alma June, who, without knowing, really taught me this:

Listen

Flowers laugh;
they really do.
Oh, yes, I know they nod and smile,
that is true;
but I said "laugh."

They share with us
the joy of sharing—
fragrance, beauty, understanding,
even bearing.
What greater sharing
than to laugh
with one another.

They even laugh
(gently, but they laugh)
when sharing with them
makes us cry.
For flowers are eternal;
they know the truth
of what it is to die,
a step into eternity with them
and God.

So share these blossoms
here with me today;
smell, and see, and touch them,
but I say,
to really share these flowers
with your other half,
for one brief spell, at least,
shut out the world
and listen
            to the flowers laugh.

March 1971

CIMMY

Cimmy's Steering Wheel

"What the hell can you say about a steering wheel?" he asked.

Well, what can one say: a ring of steel, covered by plastic? It is connected to a shaft that connects to gears and rods to control (under most conditions) the direction of travel of a car or truck. A simple and obvious definition.

But who built that wheel; what did he build it from; how did he know what size it should be, how many spokes, what diameter the rim; what must it do countless thousands of times as part of this machine (or receive as whipping post the pounding from someone caught in the merciless frustrations of our times), but always, always receive without failing?

Far back along the endless chain of human events, man discovered iron. But what iron could do only told man what a lighter, stronger metal could do, and so Bessemer half-discovered, half-invented steel.

Long before plastics became so common in our lives that they make notice only as indestructible pollutants, they were born in the minds of visionary chemical engineers. Their basic ingredients are simply those like carbon, air, and water; but it took years, and years, and more years of frustrating and costly research to discover the delicately balanced formulae that give us these nearly time-resistant building materials.

The engineer who designed this steering wheel had to draw upon the knowledge of thousands before him. He knew the wheel had to endure, without fail, the pounding and wrenching of the strongest man, yet be delicate and responsive enough for the smallest woman.

Steel, he knew, was strong enough, if properly forged and formed, to be the basic frame of this wheel; but steel is cold to the touch and would change color or rust from the acids of sweaty hands or from the oxygen and water in the air.

Plastic, though not as strong as steel, was strong enough (if he used the correct formula from the hundreds now available to him) to cover and protect the steel; it conducted heat more slowly than steel, so was less cold to the touch; and he knew it hardly cared about oxygen and water and acids and time. So he covered this steel wheel with plastic to which had been added the coloring matter that gave it that special shade that in turn "made the sale" of this car to some discriminating person.

A steering wheel: much, much more could be said about a steering wheel; but we cannot leave out here the all-pervasive fact of life and death.

For he who holds this steering wheel in his hands holds also life and death, as surely as the womb contains a life to be or the grave contains what once was living.

A simple thing, a steering wheel. Strange—isn't it?—that it also touches the beginnings and endings of man.

September 1971

To Cimmy and Rosemary

What Is a Friend?

I was hungry,
    and you fed me;
I was frightened,
    and you protected me;
I was lost,
    and you gave me direction;
I was condemned by many,
    and not all without reason,
and you stood by me.

And even if tomorrow
should find us on opposite sides
in the ideological struggles of today;
if we should find ourselves
face to face
across the battle lines
even where death
was the only move left;
even then
I could not help but remember,
you have been my friends.

God bless you both
on this, your twenty-fifth,
"as one."

December 1971

One time Cimmy really got uptight with me over something I had written. In later years I came to realize that I was wrong in what I had believed (and written), but at the time I really had to scramble to unwind him. But even through that storm, Cimmy never ceased being my friend.

TWO FRIENDS

Anchorage, Alaska
August 19, 1971

Dear Carol,

Poetry is the most compact language in the world, so it not only offers but demands many readings.

I have written poems that I myself did not really understand until years later. Others I have read years later and from them learned something that I never knew before.

So to reap the greatest harvest from any poem, read it, study it, many, many times.

I hope "Love Is . . ." strikes at least some of the chords you wanted it to.

DEAN

A little girl had asked me, one day, if I would write a poem for her
for her Mom and Dad. I asked her to make an outline for me of what
she wanted it to say. She did, and from that outline this grew:

Love Is . . .

What is love?
    Who can define it?
        Though some would divine it,
some would make it
    of the earth,
        the body,
            the senses.

All love.
    Yet no one really knows love.
        Still, love demands expression.
If all love,
    then, I love;
and *I* must express it.

I search myself for the words,
    and suddenly I see;
indefinable as that round word can be,
    that whether we share
        an intellectual discussion,
or the intimate of intimacies,
when we share
    we touch the universe,
and I know I love
    my husband.
It is through this love that I know
    I know something
of my Mother's love for my Dad.

Something indescribable and lovely
      fills me when
my husband looks at me,
      holds me,
            talks to me;

and mysterious as that word may be,
      I know that he loves
            me.
I know that I know now
      at least something
of my Dad's love for my Mother.

And children;
      a different kind of love;
yet, elusive as the definition still remains,
      when we hold our son (or let him go),
when we watch him learn and grow,
      the world is full,
            and power of the infinite is there;
and we know we love
      our son.
Can there be any question
      that now I know I know something
of the love my parents have for me?

It has taken many years;
      things of great value grow slowly;
but I am beginning to understand
      the tenderness,
            the strength,
                  the depth,
the power,
      and the wonder
            of this love;

And it is very,
      very beautiful.

August 1971

Anchorage, Alaska
May 1, 1974

Dear Lynn,

I think it would be better and certainly more honest to simply tell it like it is; that is, to say you asked someone to write the enclosed for you.

If you do decide to send it, you could tell her something like the following, or even use these words if you want to:

"Dear Mom,

"I'm not an artist, but I thought of having an artist I know do an oil painting for me to send to you. I cannot manufacture any of the thousands of articles that you would like, but I thought of carefully selecting something for you. But instead, I wanted to say something, so I asked a friend to put my feelings into words.

"Following is what I asked him to write for me.

"Love,
Lynn"

Sincerely,
DEAN NICHOLS

Dear Mom

The Bible says, "God is Love."
The unsearchable wonder that is God

is love.

How then, can I say, "I love you"?
Yet I do.

Libraries over the world are filled
with volumes on volumes of poems or essays
expressing or defining love.
Yet can love be more truly expressed

than by the faint smile of a baby
less than a few weeks old?
And I
        love you.

There are stars
billions of light-years
out into space and time
and whose message of light started toward us
before our earth was formed.
Yet in an instant
we can sweep that distance and time
into a single thought.
Here on earth you can be sitting on your porch
in the hot, Yakima sun
while I listen to the howling, forty-below wind
far up the northern slope.
Yet in that same instant of thought
you are with me in the warm glow of my thoughts;
and I am aware of the infinity
of the indescribable;
and I know
        I love you.

You who gave me birth and worry so
about that mystery so often called "my son,"
can know I share the puzzle when the fun
of some adventure steals away the glow.

So catch the silver wings that bridge the sky
and come so we can laugh, and maybe cry
a bit, about the puzzle that we share.
It could be fun, you know, and really Mom,
I care.

                              Much love,
                              LYNN

EBB TIDE

A morbid picture, perhaps, but a true one. Endure this portion of Alaska's year, and Alaska, in all her wonder and magnificence, is yours.

The Death of Winter
(A Portrait)

The Queen is dying. Long live the Queen!

Winter, the unquestioned monarch of Alaska, has reigned in all her queenly beauty for six long months. Her spotless white, her delicate and indescribably beautiful rime frost, her frosty mornings with squeaking snow, her silent nights canopied with countless beckoning stars or flashing, waving wands of northern lights, these are no more. Winter, the Queen, is dying.

Death can be serene, death can be peaceful, death can even be beautiful, but not the death of Alaska's winter. Her death is ugly, hostile, unsettled, dirty, and depressing.

One of the greatest tests of faith, the death of winter demands one look ahead down a long, long road beyond where the eye can see, and simply believe that spring is there, believe that new life comes. For when the northward moving sun strikes the first fatal blow to the heart of winter, spring is *not* just around the corner, but somewhere, somewhere down that long, long road.

Nothing less than faith can endure the days of melting, mushy snow and dripping eaves, of icy puddles in the streets, of yards that can't be cleaned because the ice is there, yet must be looked upon with all their dirt and debris, the cloudy nights when puddles freeze again and mushy snow becomes sharp ridges in the streets, and the cold is felt through your heavy coat for the first time all winter, the foggy mornings when you wonder if the sun is again going to make a slippery, sloppy, muddy mess of the surface of the still-frozen ground, or further still, raise frost heaves in stretches of good highway, or suddenly develop a bottomless pit of mud in an unpaved road.

So long held in captivity by the clean white spell of winter, we find ourselves carried along with her into sadness and depression, of longing for the old days, of struggling yet knowing the futility of struggling, of refusing to look on with faith, yet knowing we must. Winter must and will die, and we must and will go on to new life, but the parting, the sitting at the bedside of this dying monarch is a test that not all pass, and that many, many more pass only by the grace of God. This I know.

The city of Anchorage, Alaska, U.S.A. has averaged a murder roughly every ten days for the last three months, many of these accompanied by suicides. It is known that more suicides are committed in the dying weeks of winter than in all the rest of the year. More men quit their jobs or transfer outside, more talk of "home." "For Sale" signs on the houses roundabout, like pox on the sick and dying, increase in number daily, and add their morbid touch to the picture of winter's death.

This is the "portrait of winter's death"; and to be true, we must paint all the colors of the spectrum, the blacks and the browns and the bloody reds, as well as the greens and the golds and the lifting blues.

The glory of man is that he has God, and because he has

71

God, he can have faith, and if he can have faith, he can in turn have the gift of God, spring, and a new life.

It's snowing again. But look, sure enough, those are not snowflakes on those bushes outside our window.

Those are pussy willows.

April 1960

We had spent a month's vacation outside, visiting old friends and relatives, and buying a new car and driving it back up the Alcan. From here, the story explains itself.

Weariness

I am tired, I am worn, I am weary tonight.
The summer's long day left its mark.
I haven't much will for the job or the fight.
I shall welcome the cold and the dark.

And I wonder, as death of a summer is near,
and my soul and my bones cry in pain,
if the price wasn't high for the value received;
and I wonder, just what did I gain?

I have visited, traveled and seen some new lands,
and strengthened the ties to old friends;
but what of the cost to my heart and my hands?
Was it worth it, these means to these ends?

I am tired, I am worn, I am weary tonight;
and I think of the summer that's gone,
with its rush and its go and its days of no rest;
and then I smile and behold a new dawn.

September 1962

The Planting and the Harvest

I am weary, and should I be so? I have just returned from four days alone at my retreat, my cabin in the wilderness, my remedy for the ills of man. Somehow the peace wasn't there; somehow the rest never came; somehow the enveloping power of the stillness failed to wash me free of myself and the raw and oh so busy world.

That "cabin warm where a northern storm is a symphony just for you" turned out to be (this time, most unusually, I must confess) just another place of toil, another job needing to be done.

Oh, I know there is no magic in a cabin any more than there is magic in a marriage or in a doctor's office. One must give if one is to receive. One must take to the doctor's office a willingness to receive and obey instructions; one must put faith and love into marriage if faith and love you would receive; one must *take* to your cabin even that fragmentary residue of peace and rest and healing that is always there somewhere in the cup of your soul and let *it* grow as God has said even the grain of mustard seed can grow.

You cannot take burden and care and worry and strain, or that seed instead will grow. From this experience, I know.

February 1966

74

I, Too, Shall Cry

She was just a dog; seventy-five pounds of half German shepherd, a quarter Doberman, an eighth husky, and an eighth wolf. We had no pedigree certifying that, but the circumstantial evidence was all there.

Her head was small for her body, and she was a bit more concerned with food than a genteel dog should be; she was blunt, even uncouth, at times, in the way she would show affection, like climbing right up over us to get closer, when we were sitting in a chair or on the davenport, and placing her feet as carelessly as if the parts of our bodies were only parts of the furniture.

But Toni loved; she gave and received love—in quantity. Whether either of us were gone for a day or a month, her reception, her welcome home was almost painful in her struggle to express love, both giving and receiving.

When, on rare occasion, we chastened her, or if we injured her by accident, her forgiveness was total, complete, and without memory of the moment past. When, as often happens, the world seemed to reject us or count us as of no value, Toni said we were accepted and valued above all treasures.

A week ago she was young, healthy, curious, and so full of life.

This morning she died.

When Alma called this evening to share the loss with me, we talked it over awhile and tried, as always when a living part of our lives is torn away, to search the back trail trying to understand the why.

> And then there were no more words,
>   only Alma saying that she would cry.
> We said goodbye, and then, alone,
>   to God I whispered, "Yes, I know,
>
> for when my heart can hold
>   the emptiness no more,
>   I, too, shall cry."

Homer, Alaska
February 6, 1977

Chevrolet

From my Journal, Wednesday, November 2, 1977

. . . Home from midwatch at Anchorage International Flight Service Station at 8:00 A.M. Slept till noon, and then drove that grand old 1962 Chevrolet Bel Air station wagon over to Alma's job and delivered it to Buck and Charlene Stewart in exchange for a thin piece of paper worth $400.

But it wasn't quite that simple: for as Alma drove us home in the Cougar, we both noted a touch of sadness. Over a cold piece of machinery? No, that old wagon was much more. Conceived in the minds of men and created by their hand, she seemed always to carry a subtle but definite aura of life about her.

True, she was loved and cared for, but also worked and used. She was appreciated, and even thanked at times, when she performed some difficult task with again that subtle but very real extra response that loved and loyal servants do. Even as I write this, I note the suggestion of tears not far from my eyes; for when we walked away from that faithful old servant, we left behind a mute friend who will never tell the memories of the years she crossed with us.

When she came to live with us, Fred and Dean were not yet born, and Judy and Bill had not yet discovered Alaska. Jo Ann was still living at home, although awakening, with some resistance, to the fact that her father, benevolent dictator though he was, had no intention of surrendering his God-given authority in the family to democratic rule. Lloyd was living, still living that inimitable life that was so uniquely his own. And Alma and I were blissfully unaware of the terrible storms through which we were to pass and as tragically ignorant of the saving and healing power of God.

Through the ugly, painful times, through the beautiful, peaceful times, through the depression and tears, and through the laughter and joy, that steady old vehicle rolled on and on for 20-more-than-100 thousand miles. She carried the mail, and towed boats, and hauled gravel and even coal. She carried family and friends and Dutchmen and Australians and strangers, and never ever really complained.

I remember so clearly the time when, with over 90,000 miles beneath her wheels, she rolled eastward from Fairbanks for over a hundred miles at a steady 60 miles an hour and with hardly a touch on the steering wheel, and all the while with Alma sleeping peacefully by my side. I remember the almost countless times we drove her into the deep and often frozen snow and sometimes with the temperatures 30 to 40 below zero and how she struggled so valiantly and only quit when she had gone far deeper and farther than her creators had designed her to go. And even then she patiently waited, while we dug the snow away, and again, as willingly as ever, leaped to the new challenge.

It's actually silly, I suppose, to even think that cars have feelings, but the people she carried, the friends she knew, the family she served so faithfully and, if I may say, so lovingly, will always remember her and the turbulent, testing, exciting, revealing, changing, growing years her life fulfilled.

I was really depressed. A nameless sadness seemed to be pressing in from all around. I thought perhaps if I took my pen and bid it move upon the page, some truth that I could follow would emerge. Thus this "rambling."

Words

I used to gather them so easily, as others gathered flowers from the roadside, or berries from the hills, or even grain from planted fields.

> Words are everywhere, I know,
> a gift of God,
> like other growing things.

I'm sitting here, trying to shrug away my cloak of sadness so I can see the words and harvest them. And without ever knowing I exist, a tiny bird flew into my life and lifted a corner of the cloak and let a smile slip through. He wanted, and took, a drink of water, there, just outside my window, from a tiny pool I'm sure he naturally assumed (he could be right) was placed there just for him.

Here in this otherwise still-frozen land, the southward sloping roof of this house I built (just for me and mine, I thought) is gathering enough heat from the sun, 93 million miles away, to melt some snow along the eaves and drop the clear water into some exposed gravel next to my window. There, his tiny pool.

He was a Red Pole, no larger than a chickadee. He came, and drank, and let a few drops from the roof fall upon that red patch on top his head that has a hint of orange giving it a suggestion of an iridescent glow. For the briefest of moments he stood in the water with his beak slightly open while the shattered droplets spread out across his back cloaking *him* in the sparkling joy of refracted sunlight. And then he shook

himself in that fraction of time as only birds can, and flew away.
And I, because I cannot fly, return to my search for words.

>Words are everywhere, I know,
>a gift of God,
>like other growing things.

But I look out my eastern window, and nothing moves.
The snow lies cold and white and frozen upon the frozen land.
The trees are bare and lifeless, expressing not a breath of hope
that spring, and life, and leaves, and green are there, but time
away.

I look to the mountains for the words that must be buried
there and then reach into my soul for a grain of mustard seed
with which to lift their massive weight from my words. But it
is so dark inside my cloak of sadness, I cannot find anything
so tiny as a grain of mustard seed.

>I would not bring you
>dark and brooding words of sadness;
>rather would I bring you
>words of gladness,
>words of spring and life and hope and joy
>cloaking us in sparkling sunlight
>refracted from the throne of God.

And so I look to one small bird who, like the sun prying into
the edges of the snow along my roof, has lifted a corner of my
cloak of sadness and let in the sunlit promise of hope.

>Like the snow
>the cloak will go,
>the words will grow
>again for me;
>   I know, I know.

March 28, 1971

HOPE

No More, No Less

I would speak to you in words of poetry;
not necessarily in words that rhyme,
but poetry I'd sing because
it puts emotion on the wing
and lets it fly
above the fences and the walls
we build.

We need the fences and the walls
I will concede;
but now and then we need emotion freed
and flying with the wind.

Sometimes I'd speak to you
in words of sadness,
but oftentimes in words of gladness,
and passion,
    humor,
tenderness,
    and beauty too.

But all would be emotion,
generating deep within
the power that puts life in living,
the force that makes it easy
giving
of ourselves to one another.

That is all my poetry would do,
no more;
but here I must confess,
I would ever have it do
no less.

May 1971

The Bible Baptist Church in Anchorage, Alaska, needed a new and larger building. So the people, with their own hands and out of their own pocketbooks, built one.

Today, a tour through would show you a beautiful but very practical building 100 by 200 feet and housing a 1300-seat auditorium and a gymnasium, with the rest of the building split into two levels containing a cafeteria, print shop, offices and school rooms.

But that is all you would "see," rooms and lovely painted and paneled walls and carpeted floors.

Totally unseen would be the materials that hold it together and make it work.

Here in this small building are over two miles of pipe, 25 miles of wire, 50,000 board-feet of lumber, and nearly a quarter of a million nails. All unseen, these are what hold it together; these are the real structure of this building.

"Now faith is the substance of things hoped for, the evidence of things not seen. . . . Through faith we understand that the worlds were framed by the word of God, so that things which are seen were not made of things which do appear." (Hebrews 11:1-3)

I drove over to the church on the evening of December 27, 1973, feeling that somehow a word picture should be drawn; I did not know what it would be. All the framing was complete; the piping and wiring were in; but there was no paneling or plasterboard. So, for a very brief time, the building was structurally complete but exposed to be seen.

The following is what the building told me that night.

The Structure of the Universe

I stepped into a house of God tonight. No incense filled the air. There was no carpet on the floor, or hush of reverence through the room. There was no need to listen for the harmonies that choir, and string, and reed sing out to praise His holy name; they were not there. And paneling, and padded pews, and paint, and softly textured walls, and lights designed to dress them in their best, were somewhere in a storage room, forgotten, while foundation work progressed to build the basic frame.

I stepped into a house of God tonight.

A different kind of incense filled the air, and, I believe, a savor sweet rose up to please our Lord: the dust of wood, the smell of turpentine and pitch, the acrid odor of the saw as hard red fir screamed out beneath the blade.

I listened; and a joyful noise unto our Lord rang out: the saws, of course, but mostly there were hammers, hammers,

hammers driving in upon the ear the loud beginning cushioned sound of hammerhead upon the yielding nail and ending with the hard, staccato crack that tells the tender ear it is enough, enough, the nail is driven home.

I took a seat upon a box, back in the corner there beneath the balcony, and leaned against a post and looked around. The rows and rows of two-by-fours, precisely placed to answer to the scheme, rose up in such confusion that it seemed no man could claim that this was his design. And yet I know, this opportunity is mine, to see beyond the curtain we call now, to look upon one simple, single beam and know somehow that through this single one I look upon our Lord can show to me the perfect pattern of it all.

In front of me two boys were carrying some boards, some twenty feet or so and two-by-ten, and stacked them on the floor. When they were through, I stepped upon the pile and easily reached up and with my hand caressed the massive, wooden beam that keeps the balcony suspended in the air. In days to come its wonderful design will hide away beneath the paint and paneling now in the storage room. But, like the structure of the universe we cannot see, this lovely beam will carry on its work in patient secrecy.

I'm glad I came tonight and stepped into a house of God. I think, somehow, He let me slip into a favored place; I feel perhaps I should remove my shoes; this must be Holy Ground.

This is God's house, and yet I see the open studs, and joists, and beams, and pipes, and wires, and nails, and nails, and nails, and nails driven there by Christian men to hold this house in perfect answer to its plan.

For one brief moment now a vision fills my eyes; and I can see beyond the walls and night; and way out there, instead of clouds and sky and bits of light we call the stars; instead of forests and the seas and never changing mountains and the streams, I *see* that secret structure of the universe on which it all was laid.

> And as the vision fades,
>   it leaves a residue of joyous peace
>   to one
> who simply stepped into a house of God.

The Rain

O rain that falls on unjust and the just alike; o rain that serves as healing tear and washes all away our sorrow's woe; o rain that makes the grasses grow and gives the forests all their strength and size; o rain, I love thee so.

For even with your duties far and wide; with all the world to wash and feed and clothe, you take the time to tap the gentle sound upon my roof and talk to me as mother to a child.

You tell me that the world is safe and sure; you tell me that the troubles that I see are passing flashes of the storm, and it is not for me to fret and worry so. God's master plan is here at work upon the earth; and if that plan includes some pain and woe, if rank injustice seems to grow from growing fields of selfishness and greed, if raw confusion sets our minds awhirl till we cry out for some stability, then we should see God's master plan is here at work upon the earth. And though I must do what I can to ease the pain, must do my best to keep my ship square with the storm, your gentle, and sometimes your crashing, patter on my roof speaks out to me and says, "Be comforted, my son, for God's great master plan is here at work upon the earth. 'Tis not for you to fret and worry so. No matter how the storm may sweep and roar, the world is safe and sure because,

the world is in His hands."
(The rain has told me so.)

Lloyd's Pond, Alaska
July 1966

September 8, 1969

Yes, your Daddy "came up" with something on his fitieth. It was quite a tide-rip to pass through, this fiftieth. For even at forty-nine, I was still "in my forties," so the fiftieth most effectively destroyed the illusion that had become, as illusions too often do, a false reality.

But there is hope, too. My Uncle Mark was fifty-two when he and my Dad *started* the Nichols Boat Works.

Thanks for the Easter card. . . .

Love,
Daddy

Fifty

What does one do with a fiftieth birthday; celebrate or ignore it; cry or laugh over it; look backward or forward from it; see it as a peak from which the only road is down; or see it as a depth from which the only road is up?

Well, I reckon I'll neither celebrate nor ignore it; but there most surely will be both tears and laughter as I pass through it; for the view from here is clear, and the look back down the trail will be long and deep.

It has been a real climb to this place; and although I can see much and far as I look backward and downward, I have but to turn halfway around and look forward and upward with wonder and curiosity and anticipation. For this cannot be a peak from which the view ahead would be as clear as the road behind; there would then be no exhilarating unknown. And it cannot be a depth. For that would mean that this past half-century was a "down-hill-pull"; no man could stand a road that was uphill by comparison.

So I'll just see it as a plateau on which to rest a bit, regroup forces and materials, make plans, and begin the final assault on that great peak, death and eternal life.

> I wonder,
>   what is there
>   just over that next rise;
>   what will the fifty-first year bring?

September 4, 1969

The Last Step

Love starts like the spirited crackling
of cedar kindling on an early morn.
But it must be fed with harder woods
to become a fire.
And still, that's not enough,
for what is fire but a force
that must be fed, or it will die.

No, that won't do.
It must expand and cool and spread
to become a bath of water, warm
and all-encompassing.
But then, that, too, can cool,
evaporate in air, and so
the growing thing called love
must change again
and find fore'er its real source of power.

For,
like the earth and all that's life thereon
must know the sun,
so must a love attach itself to One
Who knows no death, no end.

February 1964

For Peter

Electricity, light, heat, gravity, magnetism: five fantastic wonders man so casually accepts and uses as if, of course, he knows what they are, and understands them. He doesn't, you know. He does not know what they are, and he understands only so very little about them. Here and there he puts them to work a bit, because he stumbled onto a very small part of God's infinite puzzle.

He found, for example, that he could move a metal wire through an invisible field he called magnetic (because he observed a few of the things it would do) and energy moved through the wire. He called the energy electricity, though he could not see it, truly define it, or really understand it.

But from this simple discovery, he built, for a manchild, a fair little inventory of toys and tools; enough to lead him to really believe he knows all about all five great wonders, and so accepts them so casually.

But then one says, "I have been thinking much, in the last few weeks, of an old and beloved friend I haven't seen or heard from for far too long a time."

The casual observer asks, "So?"

"Well," one answers, "he has been thinking of me. I believe he has been planning to visit me. Thoughts, at least those energized by love, travel, too, you know. And they are not limited to the slow speed of light. They travel instantly and are not at all diminished by distance."

And the casual observer, who "knows all about" the five wonders, scoffs with indignation and unbelief.

Poor blind, casual, confident man.

If he knew love, really knew love, he could then, and only then, accept the five little wonders as casually as he does. Then he would truly know all about them. Then he would understand them.

But then, if he really knew love, he wouldn't need the five simple principles at all.

November 1974

Hello, Day

Hello, day.
May I use some words to say,
I love you;
but I really want to know you better.

I know
that after every night,
however dark and long,
you're here.
Sometimes,
you greet me with a robin's song,
sometimes with wind and rain;
but always,
after every night,
however dark and full of pain,
you push the night away
and say,
"Lift up your eyes and heart;
it is the day."

I hear you, day.
And increasing times,
when memory of dark and pain are dim,
your message reaches deep inside
and stirs the dormant coals of joy;
and I can play
with life
and live no other time but this,
this day.

But all too often I've allowed
the problems of this life to crowd
the joy of life away,
reliving all the night,
forgetting how to play.

So I say,
      hello, day.
May I use some words to say,
I love you,
and I'm learning how to really know you,
light and joy of life,
this day.

April 1971

My Christian Brother, or Sister

I reached for God's hand
　　and found yours;
I listened for His voice
　　and heard you speak;
I sought His face
　　and your face shown before me.

I do not make you God,
　　nor am I the Lord;
But Jesus said,
　　"Whatsoever you do even unto the least of these,
　　so have you done unto me. . . . Love you one another
　　as I have loved you."

I'm glad He gave us one another
　　till we can touch,
　　　　and hear,
　　　　　　and see
　　　　　　　　Him
　　　　face to face.

June 26, 1973

"Through a Glass, Darkly"
(I Cor. 13:12)

Mary is not a "doubter" or "one weak in the faith." She is a highly intelligent, open, inquiring person.

That is why she could say with such simple honesty, "When the storms of this worldly life swirl around me, and the visibility is nearly zero; when the reality of Jesus is nearly lost to me as I peer into the gloom, I make myself look deeply to the right and to the left and then to what little I can see of Jesus. The only honest question comes to me, 'But what is more real than He?' "

Many years ago, when I was very young, and things like powerful searchlights and jetty and buoy and range lights were almost nonexistent, I was running a tugboat on the Columbia River. It was a dark night, and my little tugboat had a huge derrick barge lashed on ahead of it. We had just rounded the Washougal dolphin a few miles above Camas, Washington.

For the next few miles the river appeared wide and safe and inviting; but I knew that hidden just beneath the deceptive surface of the water for half a mile from either shore was gravel on the right and sand on the left.

So, some years before Mary was born, I found myself, as I had so many times before on that dark river, following her wise counsel. I looked deeply to the right and to the left and then took a long, deep look straight ahead and asked myself, "Of all I have just seen, dim and shadowy as it is, what is more real?"

We delivered the barge safely to its destination before dawn.

Twenty years later I found myself in broad daylight with the wheel of a thirty-two-foot patrol boat in my hands. We were a mile or so off the Softuk entrance to the Copper River Delta east of Cordova, Alaska.

The beautiful green water of the ocean had turned to the muddy yellow of the river silt. Ahead were breakers—right, center and left. We were going in. Our only electronic aid, our Fathometer, was reading fifteen feet and dropping.

From the instructions from those who had gone before,

I lined up the peak of a mountain with the corner of a glacier. They told me we were supposed to be right. But ahead were breakers.

The sandbars between which we must pass are so low that, because of the waves and the curvature of the earth, we could not see them until we were nearly abreast of them; too late for them to be of any use in making the entrance.

Mary was now about fifteen years old, but, of course, I had never met her. And yet, again, I followed her wise counsel. I studied the breakers to the right and those to the left and then carefully those straight ahead. The ones to the right and to the left somehow had destruction in them. The ones straight ahead, though they were white and wild, spoke something nebulously different; they were saying, "Compare us with what you see around you and ask yourself, 'What is more real; where does safety really lie?'"

Fifteen or twenty minutes later, sand appeared only a few hundred yards to both right and left; deep and quiet water lay ahead.

Another ten years passed, and I found myself sitting in a chapel; and though the buzz and flow of love was all around me, my heart and mind were caught in a swirling storm. The world had been seductively calling on every side; my heart was crying, "Where is reality; where is God?"

And Mary was sitting beside me and saying, "When the storms of this worldly life swirl around me, and the visibility is nearly zero; when the reality of Jesus is nearly lost to me as I peer into the gloom, I make myself look deeply to the right and to the left and then to what I can see of Him in those around me. The only honest question comes to me, 'What is more real?'"

And following her wise counsel, I found my way safely into the harbor again.

December 1974

For Marci

Joy

(The Infallible Sign)

Do we need signs to prove
      that God is evident?
Well, of the need I do not know,
    but signs He gives,
        as when the veil was rent,
or one lone star lit up the night
    and led the Wise Men
      to a manger low.

He gives us signs
      on clear and moonless nights
when heavens blaze with glory
      from the Throne of Lights.

He gives us signs when down into
    the inner structure of the universe
our microscopes probe deep;
      and we can know
that there before our eyes
    a marvelous design speaks
      of the One who made it so.

And then He gives the greatest signs,
so sure and true, when love and joy
      provide communications keys;
and high and low, and learned and
    unlearned ones converse with ease.

For love and joy are signs
         that can't be found
               with magnifying instruments;
nor can the farthest stars
         make them appear;
nor can degrees, nor wealth,
nor low and simple life claim to employ,
exclusively, the one, unfailing sign
         that God is near.

For God is Love; and only when we love
         can He provide
               the sign of Joy.

December 1975

www.ingramcontent.com/pod-product-compliance
Lightning Source LLC
Chambersburg PA
CBHW060421090426
42734CB00011B/2397